101 Years of Living and Learning

101 Years of Living and Learning

By Marie T. Freeman with Dick Freeman

WALNUT GROVE PRESS
Nashville, TN 37211

ISBN 1-58334-031-9
UPC 19570-00162

The ideas expressed in this book are not, in all cases, exact quotations, as some have been edited for clarity and brevity. In all cases, the author has attempted to maintain the speaker's original intent. In some cases, material for this book was obtained from secondary sources, primarily print media. While every effort was made to ensure the accuracy of these sources, the accuracy cannot be guaranteed. For additions, deletions, corrections or clarifications in future editions of this text, please write WALNUT GROVE PRESS.

Printed in the United States of America
Typesetting & Page Layout by Sue Gerdes
1 2 3 4 5 6 7 8 9 10 • 99 00 01 02 03

ACKNOWLEDGMENTS
The author gratefully acknowledges the helpful support of the entire staff at Walnut Grove Press.

COVER PHOTOGRAPHS
The front cover is a photograph of Marie Tabler at age 18.
The back cover photograph was made by Marion Ward of Nashville, Tennessee. At the time that photograph was taken, Marie Tabler Freeman was age 100. She is show with her youngest son, Dick.

For my grandchildren,
Tommy, Steven, Guy, Mallarie, Bill, Becky,
Beth, Babs, Brenda, Bonnie, Criswell,
Mary Jo, and Donna

Table of Contents

A Word about Marie Freeman

My mother, Marie T. Freeman, is something of a legend in her hometown of Donelson, Tennessee. Mother is 101 years old, soon to be 102, but Father Time can't seem to catch her. She still remembers birthdays, still watches Lawrence Welk reruns, still reads her Bible each day, still recites poetry and still offers advice to anybody who is wise enough to ask for it. Mother's insights are so priceless that I am convinced it is important to leave a permanent record of her wisdom for generations to come. So with tape recorder in hand, I have captured some of Miss Marie's best tidbits of advice along with a few of her favorite quotations and verses.

On the pages that follow, Mother shares the most important lessons she has learned during more than a century of living. Along with her favorite quotations, she shares her life story, and what a fascinating story it is. Raised in the days of horse and buggy, Marie Freeman has seen the advent of the automobile, the airplane, the telephone, the radio, the television, and the computer. She's listened to firsthand accounts of the Civil War and personally lived through the horrors of two world wars. She survived the Great

Depression and then, hand-in-hand with her husband, rebuilt from scratch. And through it all, she never lost sight of the two most important things in her life: her God and her family.

Marie T. Freeman is a remarkable lady, a lady with something to say. It is my hope and belief that her words will inspire readers in the same way that her life has inspired family and friends.

Dick Freeman

Important Dates in Marie Freeman's Life

Born in Royse City, Texas .... March 8, 1897

Moves to Atlanta, Georgia .... Summer, 1908

Visits Mt. Juliet, Tennessee and
    meets Harvey Freeman .... Summer, 1915

Graduates from Girl's High, Atlanta ....June 6, 1917

Marries Harvey Freeman; Harvey and Marie
    move to Mt. Juliet, TN ....October 24, 1917

Harvey joins the Navy; Harvey and Marie
    move to Norfolk, Virginia .... December 10, 1917

Harvey discharged from the Navy; Harvey and Marie
    return to Mt. Juliet, TN .... February 13, 1919

First son, T. Harvey, born in
    Mt. Juliet, Tennessee................... February 27, 1920

Second son, Guy, born in
    Atlanta, Georgia ....August 13, 1925

Family moves to Orlando, Florida .... September, 1925

Third son, Bob, born in
    Orlando, Florida ....August 31, 1927

Fourth son, Dick, born in
    Orlando, Florida .... February 9, 1929

Family Moves to Moore County, TN .... June, 1941

Family returns to Mt. Juliet, TN .... September, 1945

50th wedding anniversary ....October 24, 1967

Harvey's death ....December 27, 1970

Marie's 100th birthday........................... March 8, 1997

Marie publishes her first book .... February, 1999

World Events During Marie Freeman's Life

William McKinley elected president 1900
Queen Victoria dies thus ending Victorian Era 1901
Wright Brothers take first flight at Kitty Hawk 1903
First silent movie opens in Pittsburgh 1905
Henry Ford introduces Model T 1908
Income tax begins 1913
Einstein publishes theory of relativity 1914
Zipper invented 1914
Panama Canal completed 1914
United States enters World War I .... April, 1917
Communist Revolution in Russia .... November, 1917
Flu epidemic kills 20,000,000 people 1918-1919
Prohibition 1920-1933
Women earn right to vote .... August 26, 1920
First regular radio broadcast .... November 2, 1920
Florida land boom ends in crash .... October, 1925
First public demonstration of television in US 1927
Charles Lindbergh crosses Atlantic .... May 21, 1927
Stock market crash - Depression ..... October 24, 1929
US enters World War II .... December 7, 1941
WW II ends and Atomic Age begins .. August 10, 1945
Chuck Yeager breaks sound barrier 1947
Man walks on moon .... July 21, 1969
Last US troops leave Viet Nam .... August 12, 1972
Berlin Wall comes down, end of Cold War 1989
Soviet Union collapses .... December, 1991

Introduction

I'm pleased that you have taken the time to pick up this little book; I certainly hope you enjoy it. The idea for this text came from my youngest son, Dick Freeman, who thought I might have a few things worth writing about — I pray he was right.

In addition to my son, who helped me organize my thoughts, I am indebted to the caring staff at McKendree Manor Retirement Center, without whose able assistance this text would have been impossible. I am also deeply indebted to my granddaughter, Mary Jo Johnson, whose book *Marie Tabler Freeman, An Unfinished Biography* has been an inspiring reminder of my days in Royse City and of my early life. I also wish to thank my grandson, Criswell Freeman, whose research allowed me to include many important quotations that helped give richness and meaning to this book. I am eternally grateful to all the members of my family, living and departed, without whose love this book — and my life — would have been incomplete. And above all, I give thanks to the Good Lord who, in His wisdom, has seen fit to give me the strength and faculties to complete this work.

As my 102nd birthday rapidly approaches, I realize that I have been richly blessed; this text is intended, in some small way, to share a few of those blessings. These quotations and verses represent the best bits of wisdom that I've been able to gather during a century of searching. I know from firsthand experience that even if you live to be a hundred years old, these ideas will work for you because they still work for me.

Marie T. Freeman

The Long Journey Home

My name is Marie Freeman. At the time of this writing, I am 101 years old. One hundred and one years is a long time to live, and it goes without saying that I have experienced things that most people have only read about in history books. This book provides me the opportunity to share a few of my favorite recollections along with a collection of meaningful quotations and Bible verses. I hope you'll find these pages entertaining and helpful.

My life began in a wonderful place, Royse City, Texas, on March 8, 1897. I was the first-born child of two loving parents, Guy and Claudia Tabler. My sister Mamie was the second addition to the family, and baby brother Newt rounded out our little clan in 1903. Royse City was a good place to grow up in 1900 — I'm sure it still is — but I'll talk more about that later. In this chapter, I want to talk about two journeys: yours and mine.

My life's journey took me from Texas to Georgia to Tennessee to Florida and finally back to Tennessee where I now live. The circuitous trip from Texas to Tennessee was truly a journey home. My mother's family first came to Tennessee on John Donelson's flat boat in the winter of 1779. The family stayed in Tennessee until 1835 when Mexico offered settlers "one league and one labor" of land (2,519 acres) just for settling there. So the wagons were loaded and Mama's family headed to what was later to become the Republic and finally the state of Texas. Succeeding generations stayed there until 1908, the year I turned eleven. My father was offered a job working for an insurance company in Georgia, so we left the horses and wagons behind and boarded a train for Atlanta.

It was from Atlanta, in the summer of 1915, that Daddy took my sister Mamie and me to a family reunion at Mt. Juliet, Tennessee. For Daddy it was a homecoming in more ways than one. We spent the week with Uncle Ben Gleaves at the "Old Home Place," a house full of family memories. This was the same house where Daddy had been born in 1873 and where his mother was born in 1854.

For the family, this trip was our journey home to Lebanon Road, the same road Mama's family stepped on when they arrived with John Donelson (although the road was only an Indian trail in 1779). Lebanon Road was to weave like a golden thread through the lives of our family for over two hundred years. And believe it or not, I still live on Lebanon Road today!

It was at that homecoming in 1915 that I met a handsome young man named Harvey Freeman, the love of my life. Meeting Harvey changed me forever: We were married, had four boys, thirteen grandchildren, and lots and lots of great-grandchildren. All these blessings came from a single trip to Tennessee...which brings me to another journey: yours.

Whether you realize it or not, you too are on the journey of a lifetime. Perhaps the signposts are not well marked, perhaps the road is rocky, perhaps the pace is slow. But even if the pace of your life seems stalled, you've still got lots of traveling to do. During one hundred and one years of living, I've learned that the best way to travel through life is one step at a time, one day at a time, counting your blessings as you go. The pages that follow offer a few traveling tips for *your* life's journey. May it be a wonderful journey indeed.

Chapter One

Life

Life is a voyage that's
homeward bound.

Herman Melville

One life — a little gleam of time
between two eternities.

Thomas Carlyle

The leaves of life keep falling one by one.

Omar Khayyám

Oh Lord, let me not live to be useless.

John Wesley

Life is a great bundle
of little things.

Oliver Wendell Holmes, Sr.

Life is either a daring adventure or nothing.
To keep your face toward change and behave like
a free spirit in the presence of fate
is strength undefeatable.

Helen Keller

All our lives, we are preparing to be something
or somebody, even if we don't know it.

Katherine Anne Porter

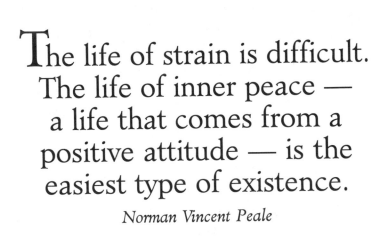

The life of strain is difficult.
The life of inner peace —
a life that comes from a
positive attitude — is the
easiest type of existence.

Norman Vincent Peale

Life is a glorious opportunity — if it is used
to condition us for eternity.

Billy Graham

Practice the attitude of putting everything
in God's hands.

Norman Vincent Peale

In all thy ways acknowledge him,
and he shall direct thy paths.

Proverbs 3:6

Seek the Lord, and ye shall live.

Amos 5:6

There is no good arguing with the inevitable.

John Russell Lowell

The best thing one can do when it is raining
is to let it rain.

Henry Wadsworth Longfellow

There is no road back to yesterday.

Oswald Chambers

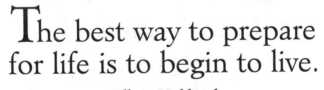

The best way to prepare
for life is to begin to live.

Elbert Hubbard

He who lives to live forever never fears dying.

William Penn

Be still, and know that I am God.

Psalm 46:10
My Husband Harvey's Favorite Bible Verse

My Childhood In Texas

In March of 1897, Royse City, Texas was a beautiful place. Life for a little girl in a small Texas town at the turn of the century was very pleasant, much like Norman Rockwell might have painted it. My world centered around family, church, school and local social events. Everybody looked forward to holidays such as the Fourth of July, Thanksgiving and Christmas. The ladies cooked for days, preparing a feast for relatives who came from far and wide. It was fun to play with cousins you only saw once or twice a year.

Social activities were a big part of my childhood, and memories of those days are still vivid in my mind. The parties at Uncle Charlie Sorrell's house were grand. It was a big house with two dining rooms and a large living room. Aunt Eva was always the belle of the ball; her parties were the talk of the town. Her home was the place where wedding receptions and church socials were held, and it was also the meeting place for a social club called the "Merry Wives of Royse." Uncle Charlie had the first car in Royse; in fact, it was the first one I ever saw.

My grandmother's house was also a fun place. We often went there to spend the night and enjoy the best vegetable soup I ever tasted. When it was time for us to go upstairs to bed, we had a little hole in the floor we could peek through and watch the grown-ups downstairs as they played cards, laughed, and talked. Friends were an important part of Mama's life. She taught us by example how to make and keep good friends. The scrapbook that friends gave her when she left Royse City was filled with wonderful poems and cards expressing their sense of loss. Ninety-one years later, I still have that scrapbook.

Over my lifetime, friends have been and continue to be one of life's greatest pleasures. I think my very best friends were my sister Mamie, whom I loved dearly, and Faith McDaniel, my very favorite high school classmate. Mamie, Faith, and countless others taught me that friendship is its own reward. In this chapter, we consider the rewards of making and keeping good friends.

Chapter Two

Friends

A friend is a present
you give yourself.

Robert Louis Stevenson

The best time to make
friends is before
you need them.

Ethel Barrymore

A friend is one who makes me do my best.

Oswald Chambers

A man cannot be said to succeed in this life who does not satisfy at least one friend.

Henry David Thoreau

You can make more friends in two months by becoming interested in other people than you can in two years by trying to get other people interested in you.

Dale Carnegie

Friendship is the only
cement that will ever hold
the world together.

Woodrow Wilson

M ake no friendship with an angry man.

Proverbs 22:24

F riendship is like money,
easier made than kept.

Samuel Butler

A doubtful friend is worse than a certain
enemy. Let a man be one or the other,
and then we know how to meet him.

Aesop

There is only one thing worse than fighting with allies, and that is fighting without them.

Winston Churchill

A friend may be reckoned
a masterpiece of nature.

Ralph Waldo Emerson

A friend is, as it were,
a second self.

Cicero

The better part of one's life consists
in his friendships.

Abraham Lincoln

The only way to have a friend is to be one.

Ralph Waldo Emerson

Any fool can criticize, condemn,
and complain — and most fools do.

Dale Carnegie

Forget flattery.
Give honest, sincere appreciation.

Dale Carnegie

Growing Up In Georgia

In 1908, Royse City was a bustling town of 1500 people. It had thirty brick business buildings, four modern churches, two banks, a weekly newspaper and an electric light plant. It also had three cotton gins that helped surrounding farmers convert their harvests into cash. Yes, Royse City was about the most perfect place I could imagine, but our family was not destined to stay there. We were moving to Atlanta.

Atlanta was definitely *not* a small Texas town — it was a real city with all the excitement we had heard about: street cars, tall buildings, theaters and massive churches. Atlanta was so much bigger than Royse that I felt a little like a fish out of water when I arrived in Georgia. At first, I terribly missed my Texas kin and friends; for a long time, I felt like a Texan away from home. But gradually I made new friends as I attended parties, church activities, dances, and picnics on Stone Mountain. We lived at 159 Sells Avenue and went to the Gordon Street Baptist Church. I later attended Girls High where I proudly graduated on May 6, 1917.

Graduation was a big opportunity for me because it meant that I was then free to marry my Tennessee sweetheart, Harvey. Our marriage, of course, was the event that changed me forever.

We all have pivotal events in our lives — whether we know it or not, we're always graduating from something. With every new transition comes opportunity. As you consider the ideas in this chapter, remember that your life is chock-full of opportunities. The following quotations can help you make your next big move.

Chapter Three

Opportunity

When one door closes, another door opens;
but we often look so long and regretfully
upon the closed door that we do not see
the ones that are open to us.

Alexander Graham Bell

A wise man will make more opportunities
than he finds.

Francis Bacon

No great man ever complains
of lack of opportunity.

Ralph Waldo Emerson

A possibility is a hint from God.

Kierkegaard

Ask, and it shall
be given you;
seek, and ye shall find;
knock and it shall
be opened unto you.

Matthew 7:7

A pessimist is one who makes difficulties out of his opportunities. An optimist is one who makes opportunities out of his difficulties.

Harry Truman

We are confronted with insurmountable opportunities.

Walt Kelly

A problem is nothing more than
an opportunity in work clothes.

Henry Kaiser

There is no security on this earth;
there is only opportunity.

Douglas MacArthur

One today is worth two tomorrows.

Benjamin Franklin

Success is a matter of never-ceasing application.

Claude M. Bristol

It took me twenty years to become an overnight success.

Eddie Cantor

Success usually comes
to those who are too busy
to be looking for it.

Henry David Thoreau

The Homecoming

The homecoming in 1915 took place at Mt. Juliet, just eight short miles east of Hermitage, Tennessee where I live today. As strange as it may seem, I was not at all excited about going to Tennessee — I had things to do in Georgia. But Daddy wanted to show off his two daughters, so to Tennessee we went. I did not dream that it was there I would meet my future husband.

The homecomng was something special: Folks from all over came back to see friends and family; some came to show off their prosperity; a few came to borrow money. Daddy was just glad to be there with my sister Mamie and me. Family ties were very important to Daddy, and he wanted us to meet his relatives. Somehow, amid the crowd, I caught Harvey's eye, later his heart, and we spent 53 wonderful years together.

Isn't it interesting how God has a plan for each of us? His plan for me was to meet Harvey at the homecoming. If you look closely at your life, you will see He has a plan for you, too. Your life will become much easier when you find God's will and follow it. I know I found His plan for me, and I pray the same for you.

Chapter Four

God's Plan

There is no limit to what
God can make us —
if we are willing.

Oswald Chambers

Life is God's novel.
Let him write it.

Isaac Bashevis Singer

Live out your life in its full meaning;
　　　　it is God's life.

Josiah Royce

This is happiness: To be dissolved in something
　　　　complete and great.

Willa Cather

I long to accomplish a great and noble task,
but it is my chief duty to accomplish small tasks
　　　as if they were great and noble.

Helen Keller

Divine Favor is unlimited
when we follow God's
recipe to gain that Favor.

Albert E. Cliffe

In His will is our peace.

Dante

.

No time is too hard for God, no situation too difficult.

Norman Vincent Peale

Said the robin to the sparrow,
"Tell me brother do you know
Why those silly human beings
Rush around and worry so?"

Said the sparrow to the robin,
"Friend I reckon it must be,
That they have no heavenly Father
Such as cares for you and me."

Anonymous

The Best Years of My Life

During the first two years of our marriage, Harvey was in the Navy. The next six years he traveled selling butter to wholesale accounts all over the Southeast. After our first child, T. Harvey, was born in Mt. Juliet in 1920, Harvey's work required constant travel. We were thankful for his job, but the traveling was difficult for all of us.

When our second boy, Guy, came along in 1925, I was at home with Mama and Daddy in Atlanta. Harvey was on the road and unable to be with us. Later that same year, Harvey had a real opportunity in Florida. It was a business that gave him a chance to travel less and spend more time with our growing family. He took it!

We bought a home at 1213 Delaney Street in Orlando. It was a beautiful little house with a shaded lot on a brick paved street. Our neighbors were the best you could ask for. It was there our two youngest sons, Bob and Dick, were born. These were happy years. We all loved Orlando, and it was truly a joy to have Harvey at home. His presence was important to me and to the boys. And of course Harvey was thrilled to spend more time with his family. Yes, those were wonderful days, and, for me, they still are. Let me explain.

You may be surprised to learn that I still spend lots of time on Delaney Street —in my mind! Those golden years on Delaney Street are, for me still very real. I think about them and even dream about them. It's always a joy for me to spend time with my memories of that happy home.

On bad days, when things aren't going right, I pick out a particularly fond memory, and I go back to Delaney Street for a little visit. Once there, I can never be sad for long. You see, those years were the best years of my life because Harvey and all four of my boys were with me. We were all at home, safe and sound. For me, that was as close as I'll ever get to heaven on earth.

Parents, take a tip from someone who knows: Remember that the most valuable time you can ever spend is the time you spend with your children. You're not only raising children, you're also making memories.

Chapter Five

Family

It takes a heap of livin' in a house to make it home.

Edgar A. Guest

A good laugh is sunshine in the house.

William Makepeace Thackeray

Happy is the house that shelters a friend.
Ralph Waldo Emerson

A true friend is a gift of God.
Robert South

Home, in one form or another,
    is the great objective of life.
Josiah Gilbert Holland

Joy dwells beneath a humble roof.
Christopher Morley

A family is a place where principles
are hammered and honed on the anvil
of everyday living.

Charles Swindoll

The crown of the home is godliness.

Henry Van Dyke

The home is God's built-in training ground.

Charles Swindoll

I have no greater joy than to hear
that my children walk in truth.

3 John:4

C hildren are the hands by which
we take hold of heaven.

Henry Ward Beecher

A happy family is but an earlier heaven.

Sir John Bowring

As for me and my house, we will serve the Lord.

Joshua 24:15

The mother's heart is the child's schoolroom.

Henry Ward Beecher

The War Years

In 1941 the winds of fate blew Harvey, me, and the boys back to Tennessee. We made it home just in time to hear the announcement that Pearl Harbor had been bombed. Someone once said that there is no such thing as a good war or a bad peace. I'm not sure about the latter, but I'm absolutely certain about the former.

As news began to flood in from overseas, I suddenly realized that war stories were nothing new to me. I'd been hearing them all my life, especially from my grandmother, Granny Tabler, who lived with us for many years. Granny was six years old when the Civil War broke out. Having experienced armed conflict firsthand, she had many stories about the horrors of war. Her tales were very real to us because she described events that happened close to home: the school yard in Mt. Juliet, the old home place, and numerous other locations up and down Lebanon Road.

At the time of Granny's death, we were living on a farm on Lebanon Road in Mt. Juliet, Tennessee within three miles of the house where she had been born. It was in Mt. Juliet that Granny raised her family, married and buried her husband and later buried all four of her children. There she lived to enjoy four generations of her descendants, and there she is buried.

Like my Granny, I've seen lots of things happen right here close to home. Today, I live on Lebanon Road, only eight miles from Mt. Juliet where my first child was born and within three miles of the home where I lived when I lost two sons, Bob and Guy. I don't pretend to understand God's reasons, but I trust Him. That trust makes my pain a little easier, but I still miss those boys every single day. Both were good men: I enjoy the memories of their childhood, and I take pride in their many accomplishments. Bob's widow, Ginny, and all of Bob and Guy's children continue to be a very important part of my life.

I did not experience Granny's war firsthand, but I did experience two of my own. I worked for the United States Navy while Harvey served in World War I and for the Army while Guy and T. Harvey served in World War II. Later Bob and Dick served during the Korean War. One of the great blessings of my life was that Harvey and all four boys came home safely from the service.

I learned from experience that times of adversity are times when we can and should grow closer to God. Whether it's a personal tragedy or the travails of war, hard times always hold the seeds for healing. The quicker we extend our hands to the Good Lord, the quicker and tighter He'll grab hold. So if you've encountered adversity, ask for God's guidance, and while you're at it, try taking the following ideas to heart.

Chapter Six

Adversity

The saints are sinners who kept on going.

Robert Louis Stevenson

Tough times never last, but tough people do.

Robert Schuller

Difficulties are God's errands and trainers,
and only through them can one come
to the fullness of humanity.

Henry Ward Beecher

Sweet are the uses of adversity.
William Shakespeare

There is no education like adversity.
Benjamin Disraeli

Be content with such things as ye have.
Hebrews 13:5

I have learned, in whatever state I am,
therewith to be content.
Philippians 4:11

Worry and anxiety
are sand in the machinery
of life; faith is the oil.

E. Stanley Jones

Anxiety is the great
modern plague.
But faith can cure it.

Smiley Blanton, M.D.

Faith can put a candle in the darkest night.

Margaret Sangster

Do not take life too seriously.
You'll never get out of it alive.

Elbert Hubbard

Yea, though I walk through the valley
of the shadow of death, I will fear no evil:
for thou art with me....

Psalm 23:4

Courage is the price
life extracts for
granting peace.

Amelia Earhart

It ain't over till it's over.

Yogi Berra

Be like a postage stamp — stick to one thing until you get there.

Josh Billings

Pray that success will not come any faster than you are able to endure it.

Elbert Hubbard

The lowest ebb is at the turn of the tide.

Henry Wadsworth Longfellow

Education is hanging on until you've caught on.

Robert Frost

When you get to the end of your rope,
tie a knot and hang on.

Franklin D. Roosevelt

Difficulties exist to be surmounted.

Ralph Waldo Emerson

The greater the adversity,
the greater in overcoming it.

Epicurus

Success is to be measured not so much
by the position that one has reached in life
as by the obstacles he has overcome
trying to succeed.

Booker T. Washington

The great paralysis of the heart is unbelief.

Oswald Chambers

So do not worry about
tomorrow; for tomorrow
will care for itself.
Each day has enough
trouble of its own.

Matthew 6:34

The Great Depression

When the radio announced the stock market crash in 1929, Harvey and I were visiting with cousin John and Pearl Glasgow at Mt. Juliet. We were having dinner when we heard the news, and we left immediately and headed home to Florida.

Harvey and I had saved and invested in National Dairies, which owned the company he worked for. In the boom of the late twenties, we had accumulated what was, for us, a fortune in stocks. In the crash, we lost it all. But Harvey did not lose his job, I did not lose Harvey, we did not lose the boys, and even though our home had a mortgage, we did not lose it. The only thing we lost was money, and in retrospect, we managed very well without it.

The only businesses that seemed to make money during the Depression were those that sold cheese and beans. You see, everybody I knew had beans for lunch and macaroni and cheese for dinner. Everything else was too expensive!

The Depression was a time of great uncertainty for everyone, and my family was no exception. But we were blessed because Harvey had a job. Many people were not so fortunate.

Even something as terrible as the Depression was not all bad. Neighbors learned to help each other; we all had to share to make ends meet. And we learned to laugh at Old Man Trouble. We could laugh because we never abandoned hope.

When tough times arrive, as they sometimes do, it's tempting to give up on the future. We see only heartache and trouble on the horizon, but the future is never as bleak as we might imagine. So if Old Man Trouble arrives at your front door, keep working, keep laughing, and above all, never give up hope. With a smile on your face and hope in your heart, you'll never stay down for long.

Chapter Seven

Hope

Now faith is the
substance of things
hoped for, the evidence
of things not seen.

Hebrews 11:1

They can conquer
who believe they can.

Ralph Waldo Emerson

Entertain great hopes.

Robert Frost

Faith is like a radar that sees through the fog.
It sees the reality of things at a distance
that the human eye cannot see.

Corrie Ten Boom

Faith can give us courage to face
the uncertainties of the future.

Martin Luther King, Jr.

Faith, if it hath not works, is dead....

James 2:17

Without faith, nothing
is possible. With it,
nothing is impossible.

Mary McLeod Bethune

The future belongs to those who believe
in the beauty of their dreams.

Eleanor Roosevelt

Make no little plans.
They have no magic to stir men's blood.
Make big plans: Aim high in hope,
and work hard.

Daniel Hudson Burnham

The thing we fear we bring to pass.

Elbert Hubbard

God is our refuge and strength,
a very present help in trouble.

Psalm 46:1

Act as though it were impossible to fail.

Dorthea Brand

Fear is the absence of faith.

Paul Tillich

Go forth and meet the shadowy future
without fear.

Henry Wadsworth Longfellow

Become so wrapped up in something
that you forget to be afraid.

Lady Bird Johnson

The first and great commandment is
don't let them scare you.

Elmer Davis

Never despair,
but if you do,
work on in despair.

Edmund Burke

I am an old man and have known
a great many troubles, but most of them
never happened.

Mark Twain

If you see ten troubles coming down the road,
you can be sure that nine of them will run
into the ditch before they reach you.

Calvin Coolidge

"Worry" is a word I don't allow myself to use.

Dwight D. Eisenhower

I will lift up mine eyes unto the hills,
from whence cometh my help. My help cometh
from the Lord, which made heaven and earth.

Psalm 121:1

Keep you fears to yourself, but share your courage with others.

Robert Louis Stevenson

All human wisdom is
summed up in two words:
wait and hope.

Alexandre Dumas

Five Years On A Hog Farm

Tough times are often opportunities in disguise, but tough times never offer us opportunities free of charge; usually we must work for them. Harvey and I learned firsthand about opportunities and hard work when, in 1941, we moved to a hog farm. Why, you ask, a hog farm? Well for years, we had lived in Orlando and manufactured a tasty product called Tennessee Farm Sausage. Ours was a small business, and we simply couldn't sell enough sausage in Central Florida to make ends meet. It was time for a change.

Harvey had gone on a business trip to Atlanta and was at the station to catch a train back to Orlando. He was sitting in the waiting room when he noticed that a train was leaving for Nashville before the one that would have taken him back to Orlando. Harvey said later that the business in Orlando seemed hopeless, and he knew he had good friends and unknown opportunities in Tennessee. On the spur of the moment, he asked the ticket agent how much it would cost to go to Nashville instead of Orlando. The agent's answer was simple: It cost nothing. So Harvey changed his plans and sought a new life in Tennessee. That small cardboard ticket, less than one inch square, changed our lives forever.

With World War II only six months away, we moved back to Tennessee. This time it was to a farm in Moore County. For the next five years, the family business was a garbage route serving Camp Forrest, an Army base located just outside a small town called Tullahoma. We fed as many as 2,500 hogs on leftovers from the camp's mess halls. It took a lot of hard work, three large trucks and hundreds of 32-gallon cans to pick up the garbage each day. The garbage was poured onto large concrete slabs, all of which had to be cleaned after every feeding. The garbage cans were washed in boiling lye water. Then the cans were returned to camp empty and exchanged for full ones the next morning. Every day that the soldiers and the hogs ate we worked. That turned out to be 365 days a year.

During those five years, Harvey paid off his debts, and we saved enough money to start over. When the war ended, we were almost as happy as the soldiers who were coming home.

In some ways, the war years were wonderful years. Our two older boys, Guy and T. Harvey, survived the war. Harvey and our two youngest boys, Bob and Dick, worked very closely together. Although we had no running water or electricity, we never missed a meal or even came close. We had wonderful neighbors, good schools and churches. I cooked for the family and for as many as 20 farm hands. One summer I canned 108 quarts of blackberries. I lost count of the cans of green beans, tomatoes and apples. The entire family learned much from the experience of living on a hog farm, and my memory is crowded with all the good times we had together.

The best of times for you may come when you least expect them. In our case, a hidden blessing came from our return to Tennessee. Three of our boys met wonderful Tennessee girls who blessed me with beautiful grandchildren and great-grandchildren. How's that for dividends on a failed business and five years on a garbage route?

If life ever finds you on the back end of a garbage truck, keep smiling and keep working. Experience tells me that you'll find blessings whenever you decide to look for them *and* work for them.

Chapter Eight

Work

When troubles arise, wise men go to their work.

Elbert Hubbard

Think enthusiastically
about everything,
especially your work.

Norman Vincent Peale

Make the work interesting and the discipline
will take care of itself.

E. B. White

Do your work with your whole heart
and you will succeed —
there is so little competition.

Elbert Hubbard

The reward of a thing well done
is to have done it.

Ralph Waldo Emerson

When your work speaks for itself,
don't interrupt.

Henry Kaiser

There is not only utility in labor,
      but also beauty and dignity.

Booker T. Washington

Everywhere in life, the true question
      is not what we gain, but what we do.

Thomas Carlyle

The world cares very little about what a man
or women knows; it is what the man or woman
      is able to do that counts.

Booker T. Washington

It is better to wear out than to rust out.

Bishop Richard Cumberland

Well done is better than well said.

Benjamin Franklin

Do noble things, do not dream them
all day long.

Charles Kingsley

All work is seed sown; it grows
and spreads itself anew.

Thomas Carlyle

Thank God every morning when you get up
that you have something which must be done,
whether you like it or not. Work breeds
a hundred virtues that idleness never knows.

Charles Kingsley

When love and skill work together, expect a masterpiece.

John Ruskin

By their fruits
ye shall know them.

Matthew 7:20

Fifty-Three Years With Harvey

I have often been asked what was the best thing that ever happened to me, and I have never hesitated in answering. It is not even a close call. The best thing that ever happened to me was marrying Harvey and having his children.

From the first time we met, we both knew that we were destined to be together. During our courtship, we wrote to each other, and he made trips to Atlanta. On October 24, 1917 we were married at my parent's home at 67 Lawton Street in Atlanta. Our wedding was small: My family was there and Harvey's brother Charles came from Tennessee. Harvey and I left Atlanta right after the ceremony. Our honeymoon was the trip to Mt. Juliet where we took up residence at the Freeman's boarding house, the "Freewood." Harvey got up the next morning and went to work across the street at the Bank of Mt. Juliet. He was assistant cashier, and his salary was $10 a month. Not much, but enough.

We lived in Mt. Juliet until Harvey joined the Navy and we moved to Norfolk, Virginia. Harvey was a yeomen in the paymaster's office, and I took a job as a civilian employee of the Navy.

In a way, our time in Norfolk was our real honeymoon, but in truth, the honeymoon lasted 53 years. We hardly had a cross word, and the tougher the times, the closer our family became. Somehow it seems easier to be truly thankful when times are lean than when the harvest is bountiful. I think one secret of our happy marriage was that we learned to love and appreciate each other no matter what the circumstances.

God was good to me when He put me on that train to Mt. Juliet to meet Harvey. Our journey together included two years of courtship and 53 years of marriage. It was a journey that took us through lots of times, some good and some not so good. But we always had each other, and that was always enough. Harvey has been gone 28 years. To this day my most treasured memories — and my fondest dreams — are of our years together.

On your journey, have fun, work hard, and build good memories. And above all, remember that love makes the journey worthwhile.

Chapter Nine

Love

Life is the flower of which love is the honey.

Victor Hugo

Love is a great beautifier.

Louisa May Alcott

Love is multiplication.

Marjory Stoneman Douglas

Love is the essence of God.

Ralph Waldo Emerson

And now abideth faith, hope, love, these three; but the greatest of these is love.

I Corinthians 13:13

Love stretches your heart
and makes you big inside.

Margaret Walker

Of all the earthly music, that which reaches
farthest into heaven is the beating
of a truly loving heart.

Henry Ward Beecher

The giving of love is an education in itself.

Eleanor Roosevelt

Love is, above all, a gift of oneself.

Jean Anouilh

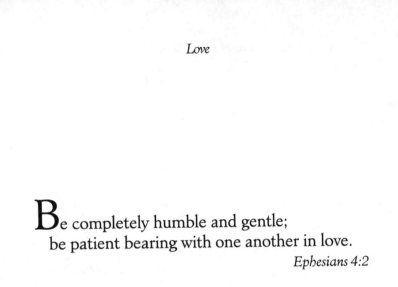

Be completely humble and gentle;
be patient bearing with one another in love.

Ephesians 4:2

Whoever loves true love will love true life.

Elizabeth Barrett Browning

There is only one terminal dignity — love.

Helen Hayes

Bitterness imprisons life;
love releases it.
Bitterness paralyses life;
love empowers it.

Harry Emerson Fosdick

Love is responsibility.

Martin Buber

Love and you will be loved.
   All love is mathematical, just as much
   as the two sides of an algebraic equation.

Ralph Waldo Emerson

Love seeks only one thing:
   the good of the one loved.

Thomas Merton

To get the full value of joy, you must have someone to share it with.

Mark Twain

The best and most beautiful things in the world cannot be seen or even touched. They must be felt with the heart.

Helen Keller

Those who love deeply
never grow old;
they may die of old age,
but they die young.

Sir Arthur Wing Pinero

When the evening of this life comes, we shall be judged on love.

Saint John of the Cross

The Golden Years

After Harvey's death in 1970, when I was seventy three years old, my life became very different. I was a widow. And I was lonely.

It seems to me that long widowhood is a tradition in our family. My mother survived my father by 25 years. My grandmother, Granny Tabler, survived my grandfather by 29 years. Both Mama and Granny were living with me at the time of their deaths. As the years have gone by, I have felt a greater closeness with both of them. Having walked in their shoes, I now know how they felt. My mother and grandmother survived with grace and dignity and continued to contribute to the lives of their children, grandchildren, great grandchildren and a host of relatives and friends. They learned to move beyond their grief and be thankful for the blessings they enjoyed.

God is in the business of opening doors: Whenever one door closes, God is standing by another door, beckoning us to enter. But the moment we become embittered is the moment we lose sight of our opportunities.

All of us are blessed. We have countless opportunities to help others and to contribute to the lives of our families and friends. Even in the most difficult circumstances, we can always find ways to contribute to a world that badly needs our help. So even if your heart is breaking, take time each day to give thanks. When you do, you'll discover that even on the darkest day, a door is open to you. The Good Lord loves a thankful spirit, and every day is Thanksgiving Day *if* you're wise enough to count your blessings.

Chapter Ten

Thanksgiving

Enter into his gates
with thanksgiving and into
his courts with praise:
be thankful unto him
and bless his name.

Psalm 100:4

May silent thanks at least
     be given to God with a full heart;
     Our thoughts are heard in heaven.

William Wordsworth

Cultivate a thankful spirit!
     It will be to you a perpetual feast.

John R. MacDuff

We should spend as much time in thanking
     God for his benefits as we do
          in asking for them.

Vincent De Paul

I thank God for my handicaps; for through them, I have found myself, my work, and my God.

Helen Keller

Gratitude is the sign of noble souls.

Aesop

Plenty of people miss their share of happiness,
not because they never found it, but because
they didn't stop to enjoy it.

William Feather

Gladly accept the gifts of the present hour.

Horace

So much has been given to me, I have no time
to ponder over that which has been denied.

Helen Keller

Happiness doesn't depend upon who you are
or what you have; it depends
upon what you think.

Dale Carnegie

Life is what we make it.
Always has been.
Always will be.

Grandma Moses

He that is of a merry heart
> hath a continual feast.

Proverbs 15:15

Laugh and the world laughs with you.
> Weep and you weep alone.

Ella Wheeler Wilcox

The mind is like a clock that is constantly
running down. It has to be wound up daily
with good thoughts.

Bishop Fulton Sheen

So it is with cheerfulness:
The more of it is spent,
the more of it remains.

Ralph Waldo Emerson

This is the day which
the Lord hath made;
we will rejoice
and be glad in it.

Psalm 118:24

Words to Another Generation

In February of 1999, the Lord willing, my first great-great grandchild will be born. My great-granddaughter Reshal is expecting a baby, and I plan to be here for the event. A new generation of our family will begin.

There is much that each of us would like to pass on to future generations. After considerable thought, I would like to do just that, to share a few words with present and future generations. So here they are, some of the most important lessons I've learned during 101 years of living.

Chapter Eleven

Advice

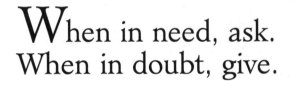

When in need, ask.
When in doubt, give.

Stay interested in everything and everybody.
It keeps you young.

Even if you live to be a hundred,
never stop seeing the world
through a child's eyes.

Take time every day to laugh and to pray,
but not necessarily in that order.

Trust in God. Even if you fail Him,
He will never fail you.

Live honestly and always tell the truth.
Especially to yourself.

Forgive early and often.

Expect miracles.

Stay away from
fatty foods, hard liquor,
and negative people.

Do the unpleasant work
first and enjoy the rest
of the day.

A little hard work never killed anybody,
but too little hard work has sure made plenty
of people miserable.

Do what's expected of you and
then do a little more. That little extra effort
makes all the difference.

Never fail to do something because
you don't feel like it. Sometimes you just
have to do it now and feel like it later.

God has a plan
for your life.
Search for that plan
quietly every day.

Look for the good
in everybody, starting
with yourself.

Remember that you're never alone because wherever you are, God got there first.

And finally, take good
care of yourself.
Somebody's going to live
to be a hundred, and it
might as well be you.

Love,
Marie T. Freeman

Sources

If you enjoyed this book, you'll enjoy other inspirational quotation books from Walnut Grove Press.

For information about other titles, please call 1-800-256-8584